Illusions
of Truth

A collection of intriguing poems
based on truth and deceit.

To my Friends Chris and Joan.

by
Ronnie Bee

Ronnie Bee

Published by:

Honeybee
Publishing Company
P.O. Box 941
Douglasville, GA. 30133-0941
First Edition
First Printing • 500 • March 1997

Library of Congress
Catalog Card Number: 97-93103
ISBN - 1-57502-438-1

Additional copies may be obtained by sending a check for $12.^{95} to HoneyBee Publishing Co., at the address above, (*Includes Postage & Handling, Georgia residents add 6% sales tax*). An order form can be found at the back of this book for your convenience.

Illusions of Truth may be purchased at special rates for multiple copies, Write to the above address for more information.

Printed in the USA by

*M*ORRIS
PUBLISHING

3212 E. Hwy 30
Kearney, NE 68847
800-650-7888

INTRODUCTION:

Illusions of Truth is a compilation of some of my favorite poems I have penned over the years. This particular volume is based on the idea of truth and deception. How do we know when our dearest friend, spouse, or even an esteemed author is telling us the real truth.

Are all persons truly created equal? (Uh hummm, perhaps;) At least at birth, we are all born equally *untrained*, if nothing else.

Then begins the learning process. As soon as we learn enough to leave our diapers behind and begin wearing training pants, we begin to realize we are not perfect. We make mistakes. People are usually ashamed when they err. Soon we begin to try and cover our mistakes with deception.

"Ronnie, did you draw on the wall with your crayons!"

"No Ma'am, I was outside playing."

And sometimes we even to begin to deceive ourselves.

Thinking, "It was *the crayon* that *left the mark* on the wall, *not me!* I mean, just because I was holding on to it doesn't make me guilty, does it?"

I'm exaggerating of course, but you see the point. Our outward appearance—the innocent look—the counterfeit speech, are all part of a mask. This mask is an illusion that covers the nude spirit of the real, inner-self, personality.

There are many other reasons people use deception other than covering guilt: We use it to:

- Gain illegal profit
- Manipulate people
- Exaggerate, (brag)
- Keep from hurting those we love

Etcetera, etcetera, etcetera.

Deception comes in many forms: white, black, and gray. As you peruse the pages of this collection, will you be able to sift the truth from illusion? I would hope so.

Ronnie Bee

Poetry
*Poetry—rhymed verse
Played on instruments of id
Music of the soul.*

This volume is dedicated to,

Lady Grace
and
Our Children

Also

To the Memory of
My Good Friend

John D. Kirkland

Whose inspiration and
encouragement led me
to greater heights.

INDEX

INDEX

Illusions of Truth

Illusions of truth—masks of deception
Cover the nudity of shameful sin,
To hide the heart from prying inspection
That would discover negatives within.
Oh would that love would teach us her wisdom
And set us free from loathsome lust and strife,
So we could live in a peaceful kingdom
Shunning the ways of death and choosing life.

If only we were equal to this task:
To lay deceit aside and let it be,
Then all mankind could shed their shameful masks,
And understand why truth can set us free.
*   I say "Deceit! I wish you void and null"*
*   That we may see the nude and beautiful.*

Stargazer
[*A Traditional Sonnet*]

What are you searching for, oh man of earth?
You stand upon the mountain-tops and gaze—
Hoping to find perhaps that source of birth,
From whence the light was born in splendorus blaze?
The secrets of our universe are kept
Within the pages of a book called time—
In cryptic messages that eons slept
Inside the vaults of keepers undefined.

Spirits, will awake on some future date,
After Father Time's cosmic clock has turned—
And pointed out the entrance to the gate
That leads to paradise, a gift unearned.
   Then, man will know the truth that eons slept,
   And understand the reason why God wept.

Fall

The smell of wood-smoke
Fills the air.
Small furry food hunters
Scurry here and there.
Leaves turning crimson,
And birds flocking everywhere,
Hear whispers in the wind
Saying "Winter's coming here."

Summer is over.
We can sure tell
By the compelling tone
Of the clanging school bell.
The chill of morning
Makes long sleeves feel swell,
And blowing leaves whisper,
"Fall just now fell."

Old House

[***To Judy & Wayne,***
whose 1890 home inspired this work.]

I love to discover an old house
And trod its creaking hallowed halls
Where transient ghost from days gone by
Flit past the faded papered walls;
As some long forgotten deed or word
Floats by when memory recalls.

The musty fragrance of time worn drapes
Blends with aromas of fresh new paints
And cleaning soaps with oil of pine
To wash away the mildew's taints
From ancient glass and antique wood
On pictures of departed saints.

Grandfather Travis looks fearless and bold.
The gleam in his eye speaks merriment and mirth,
And sweet aunt Mercy—peaceful looking soul;
She gave her young life bringing Bonnie to birth;
Midst other kith and kin all noted in the Holy Book—
All resting now 'neath the churchyard's still earth.

If this house could tell its handsome tale
Of souls passed on through history's haze;
It would give our hearts a thrill
As it told the deeds of bygone days.
And picked the bones of closet skeletons
Brought from secret passageways.

Let's take time out from life's dull chores
As this old world spins by so fast,
To repair the stately sagging wood,
So awhile longer the old house will last.
Lets fill our minds with memories of its lore,
And so recapture the glories of the past.

A Silent Friend

There are nice words that we can say
That create good from day to day;
Promoting peace with joy and love,
They fall like raindrops from above.
But other words can bring out rue,
And when they're said, make war ensue.
They call for hate and pain and strife,
The ways of death instead of life.

We should consider every word,
And those by whom it might be heard.
Will they receive them joyfully,
Or could it make an enemy?
Give pause, and think before you speak;
Is friendship what your words would seek?
Sharp words, like knives, cut to the bone,
And make us want words to atone.

How oft this wish must we repeat—
Bring back the words I said in heat.
Until we learn from this day hence
To overlook each small offense.
So, if it's peace I would pursue,
Before I speak, I'll think of you.
And if Ill will those words would spread,
'Tis better they remain unsaid.

Riding On Pale Colored Horses

Come ride with me on a pale colored horse
From the eastern gate o'er the rainbow's crest.
Through the halls of time on a lifelong course
To the place where the sun sets in the west.
Searching for knowledge and wisdom divine,
We create our world with these mental tools.
We love, we hate, we put life on the line.
Are we "human gods", or just mortal fools?

Like steeds of awareness set loose from id
Our minds journey on from daybreak to night
To destinations beyond which are hid,
Unknown fortunes in celestial light.
*   Call it light, or dark, whatever you will;*
*   We'll know for sure when the body lies still.*

Lady Grace

Martha Ann is your name,
It means "*Lady Grace*,"
But to me it means love
When I see your sweet face.

You're a "*Lady*" for sure,
My companion for life.
God has answered my prayer
For a pure loving wife.

God has given me "*Grace*"
Sent from heaven above.
He has bound us together
Forever in love.

*[Dedicated to: Martha Ann
On her birthday, May 26, 1982]*

Milady

I sought true love
Among the stars,
And in expressions
Of earth's face
I kissed the Moon,
And woo'ed the Sun,
But then I married
Lady Grace!

Silver Anniversary

How wonderful! How glorious!
Our Silver Anniversary.
I yearn for words to let you know
How very much it means to me.

My heart is filled with tender thoughts,
Remembering the times gone by.
We met in may—among the flow'rs—
Love bloomed beneath a summer sky.

Midst falling leaves we made our vows
And wintered in a sheltered lee.
My life was filled with untold joy
Knowing God gave you to me.

My wife, you are my greatest prize,
Because your love has never failed.
Though there were times I made you cry—
You stuck by me—our love prevailed.

O'er these years I've come to know
Marriage is made to last life through.
Oh what a blessing it has been
To have a lovely wife like you.

The Lord of Life brought us this far,
So as his plans for us unfold,
Cherish our silver gift of love,
And watch it slowly turn to gold...

[I wrote this for Martha Ann on our, (twenty fifth,) Silver Anniversary. I had it copied in calligraphy and mounted in a silver frame. It now hangs in a place of honor on our living room wall.]

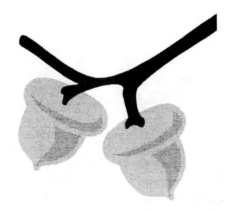

The Boy From Oak Hill

I left the courtroom saddened
  By the judge's deft decree,
Though from alcoholic parents
  His rule had set me free.
He placed me in the county home,
  A place they called Oak Hill.
I soon adjusted to their ways,
  And have fond memories still,
Of wild and reckless welfare teens,
  In bobby sox and rolled up jeans.

I still see twilight summer scenes—
  Me! Kissing girls through window screens.
Hands on the sill—warm brick and cement—
  Catching the sweet delicious scent
Of fresh cut, dew kissed grass;
  Then, almost getting caught and running fast.
Flyin' cross the hill to the big boys house.
  Sneakin' to bed Like a scared little mouse.

20

Dawn and breakfast come too soon.
  I turn around, it's nearly noon!
We station wagon over to the city park—
  Jukebox blastin'—we swim till dark.
Going home, painted toes rest on my own bare feet.
  There's beauty in my lap for lack of car seat.
Damp Suit—The smell of chlorine from the pool—
  Arm 'round her trim waist, tryin' to keep cool.
She smiles. The wind from the window
  Blows her corn-silk hair.
The scent of honeysuckle fills the air.

Unload the wagon—Go check the mail—
  Wash up for supper—Can't wait for the bell.
Set the five tables, each one will hold four.
  Put out the food and open the door.
Stampeding boys scramble
  Quick to their place.
Housemother—head table—
  Bids us "shush", for the grace.
Dive in—Hurry! If you want seconds,
  Wolf down your food;
Then off to your room
  For a quiet interlude.

Fourteen Kids in the station wagon packed,
  I'm riding shotgun, back seats are stacked.
We're off to the Starlight drive-in show.
  With fifty-cents allowance, saved from weeks ago.

Wood benches—A concrete deck—
  A sweet young thing hung 'round my neck.
A secret kiss in the moonlight's silvery glare.
   No worries—No sorrows—No future care.
Young—Strong—Full of romance—
   Missing most of the movie watchin' fireflies dance.

Looking at cars—
   Turning green with greed.
In the high school boys room
   Puff a hot boxed weed.
Here a dime, there a dime,
   Save it for awhile.
I need a blue suede jacket
   To really be in style.

Lunch money thirty five—
   A quarter for smokes—
A nickel for potato chips—
   A nickel for a cokes.
After school—Waiting—
   Telling dirty jokes.
Waitin' for the weekend—
   Going to see my folks.

Thanksgiving—Waitin' at the front gate—
   Ask the new girl's name.
The Legionnaires are coming
   To take us to the game.
They ride a big parade train
   That doesn't need a track.
They'll pick us up and take us

22

To the football game and back.
Push and shove to grab the engine—
 We can wave and look so swell,
But comin' back the boxcar's best,
 At night that engine's colder'n hell.
They will come back Christmas
 And take us to their Hall.
Good ol' American Legion; they provide a tree,
 Lots of turkey, and Christmas gifts for all.
Appreciation—Grateful—
 Here's to those Legionnaires who cared.
For the hope they provided,
 And the moments we shared.

The winter air is bitter cold;
 The wagon's like a fridge.
Park it here, we'll find a spot
 Beneath the crystal bridge of
Glass and steel that spans the arch
 High above the street—
Holding hands beneath her coat—
 Trying not to step on feet.

Level one lights up—Oh Look!
 Behind the glass—A choir.
Their song drifts down on upturned faces.
 Two, Three, and Four light up, and
Now at last we're waiting still and patient,
 For the lighting of the great tree.

We join in the singing and
  Our eyes are damp with tears, as
We contemplate the Christ Child
  Reaching out across the years.
Homeward bound—Street-lights
  Passing in the dark—
Snuggle close—
  Soon our hands are warm as toast.

Flowers bloom—Tree buds sprout—
  Off with the shoes—School is out!
Back to the woods—
  Playing softball on the lawn—
Three boys were lost to service—
  Two girls have gone back home.
We remain to greet replacements,
  To test their mettle and their grit.
We'll learn their secrets by acquaintance;
  We'll see exactly where they fit.

Then one day the bags are packed;
  My room is cleaned and given a fresh coat of paint.
Funny how the house-mother
  Suddenly seems almost a saint.
Soon the bus will come
  To take me back to town.
This summer day the oaks are still
  As I walk once more across the hill
  For just one more look around.

The last five years of my life
  Have Been spent on this hill.
Now it's ending—
  My tears start to spill.
But, then I think, "my life is just beginning—
  Yes! Out there my fate awaits."
Smiling, I turn and wave,
  And walk out through the gates...

[*The events in this poem occurred at Oak Hill Homes, Where I was a ward of Fulton County, Atlanta, Georgia from 1952 through 1957, between the ages of 12 to 17. A very memorable period in my life.*]

The Promise in the Light

I gazed upon a waterfall
Hid in a fragrant wood.
The misty crystal droplets formed
A pool whereby I stood.
Above the golden sunlight cast
A rainbow in the spray.
Its colors spilled upon the Rock
In hues of rich display.

I felt a holy presence there
So close that I could hear,
A silent witness in my soul
Say "God himself is near."
Then flowing love embraced my heart
In that secluded wood;
While time stood still as I beheld
And clearly understood.

Here, is the promise made to man!
Who dwells within the clay.
The beauty of the broken light
Speaks of another day.
A day when love will rule the earth
And man will be God's friend;
Then pain and death will be no more,
And time will have no end.

Real Love Will Never Say Good-bye

There is a place of boundless joy
  Illusive lovers never find;
Beyond the realm of earthly cares,
  That occupy the worried mind.
We found that place of joyful bliss
  The day we gave ourselves away—
Two gifts of rare and holy love
  Presented on our wedding day.

Because we trusted in our love
  To keep our union free from sin,
That love protected us from harm
  And evil strife that would creep in.
When we're apart, we do not grieve;
  But keep our sights on things unseen,
Knowing our love is bound by faith,
  No distant miles can come between.

Though we are separate; we're still one—
  Our spirits locked in loves embrace,
And joy abounds when we return
  To tender kisses face to face.
If I am first to leave this earth,
  My darling sweetheart, do not cry;
For in the language of real love
  There are no words to say good-bye.

The Last Enemy

I have an enemy out there
   Lurking in the shadows
   Of some year, month and day.
The exact time and place I cannot say,
   But I know a sure appointment
   Has Been made for us to meet.

I walk in a valley of shadow,
   Hearing his footfalls close by my side.
Yet I will not fight, struggle, or resist him.
When my time comes I'll seek no place to hide.

I must not worry about his attack.
I will not cringe with deep inner strife.
My hope is in love, the substance of life.

Someday you will come and strike your cruel blow.
My body will lie 'neath the shade of some stately tree.
But my spirit, Released! will suddenly be free.

I will put off my old life and put on the new.
When the battle is over, I'll have defeated you.
Nothing else can you harm—Nothing else can you do.

So bide your time my foe of destruction
'Till the swift moving days have flown past.
When your time has come and gone, you're the last.

The Great Shepherd

A hundred sheep were in his fold;
He called them all by name,
He kept them fed and watered well—
Cared for the sick and lame.

He led them beside still waters,
To abundant pasture land.
The best of it the sheep received
From this Great Shepherd's hand.

Returning from a mountain stream.
A lamb was left behind.
When the shepherd counted them,
His tote was ninety nine .

"My Stars!" the gentle shepherd said,
"A lamb of mine is lost.
I must go at once and look for it,
No matter what it cost."

He left the ninety and the nine,
And searched both far and near,
Until he found that poor lost lamb,
Beset by wolves, trembling in fear.

The shepherd blew a trumpet blast
To scare the wolves away,
With his hands picked up the lamb,
And rescued it that day.

Now, when the shepherd comes again,
The sheep will all rejoice,
Because he found that poor lost lamb,
They'll join his singing voice .

They'll praise the shepherd for his love,
The love that sets them free;
I'm so glad the shepherd cares,
That poor lost lamb, was me.

Passing Shadows

This is not the real world
We are living in.
These are slowly passing shadows
Of a world that might have been.

The earth is clothed in beauty
In everything we see,
Except for waste and painful death
That afflicts humanity.

But these are shadows surely passing,
Fleeting clouds that hide the sun,
Shrouds of gloom that will be gone,
Once real life has begun.

Instruct my heart in ways of love,
So the Sun may light my way.
To walk the path of perfect light,
On a fair and brighter day.

I realize this present world
Is turning into rust.
But I can see beyond the shadows,
When I teach my heart to trust.

And I'm convinced tomorrow,
Will be a brand new day
Awaiting those who have believed,
Once shadows pass away.

If we believe, does death become
A gate to...life eternal?
We know all souls must surely pass
That secluded, puzzling portal.

But, as you pass that loathsome gate,
Remember please, these words I say.
When you have faith, then I believe,
You'll find all shadows passed away.

The Show Is Over

Once again the lights grow dim
And images begin to swim
As curtains rise up off the floor
Revealing there a magic door—
The silver screen above the stage
Where lovers court and battles rage.

In *Fifty One, for one thin dime,*
A boy like me could have a time
Escaping pressures brought to bear
By poverty and earthly care—
Mid tales of daring, love so pure,
And tragedies heroes endure.

The plot unfolds, romance blooms,
As I explore mysterious rooms,
Or ride a fast fictitious train
While music scores entice my brain.
I lust for wealth and fancy cars,
My eyes caressing female stars.

Chills creep up my back in fear
When fiends from outer space appear.
Nerves tense up along my spine
While U.D. teams disarm a mine.
I squirm and hold my popcorn tight
As the show continues in the night.

"THE END" appears, and the silent sound
Brings the final curtain down.
The good guys triumphed o'er the bad,
Yet as I leave my heart is sad,
Knowing cares I left at the ticket booth,
I must pick up, and face the truth.

[*From 1949 to 1952, I attended every Hollywood movie that was a major hit. Admission for under 12 years old was ten cents, and I looked young for my age. This was my form of escapism for one of the worst periods in my early life.*]

35

A Whistling in the Rain

One coal black night in a drizzling mist,
On a dark secluded lane,
From a graveyard's cold gray stones there came
A whistling in the rain.

A haunting spectral melody
Floating on the chill night air
Just loud enough to catch my ear,
And set my bones a trembling there.

A ghostly couple slowly rose
From the graves in locked embrace.
Their forms like moonlit waters danced,
In liquid stately grace.

The whistling swelled up once again
Pale fingers on the fife,
Piped on the dirge for love-bound souls
Lost in serene ethereal life

The ghostly couple, young and fair,
Embraced in pale moonlight,
Pledging timeless love and promises—
What an awesome, eerie sight.

Then breaking dawn erased that scene.
The sun warmed cold hard ground.
I found these words carved in a stone,
And learned that they had drowned.

In Nineteen Hundred Twenty Eight
Tommy Brown, & Sue Anne Blake,
1904 - 1928   1907 - 1928
Set Sail Upon a Stormy Night,
And Died in Sutter's Lake.

Or did they find eternal love?
The musing teased my brain.
I see them ever dancing when,
There's a whistling in the rain

Colors of Life

God, when you left your regal throne
　To visit us on earth,
Your love was manifested in
　A tiny baby's birth.
Just a Noah, the man of old,
　Saw light pass through the clouds,
And form a sparkling rainbow in
　Their high and misty shrouds;
Your light passed through the waters of
　This world before men's eyes,
And broke into a promise of
　A life that never dies.

Red shows your love, a love so great
  You shed your blood for me.
Green tells me of the awesome price
  That bought my liberty.
Blue whispers of your body bruised
  And ugly stripes you bore.
You wore a crown of cutting thorns
  To heal my every sore.
Soon Calvary brought silver tears
  And agony your way;
But then bright yellow sunshine broke
  The dawn on Easter Day.

You left the grave victorious
  With keys of death and hell,
To gain the golden crown of life,
  And sit down for a spell
Beside God's purple majesty
  To wait for that great day
When God will wipe away all tears
  Along with black and gray.
Then darkness cannot enter in,
  All will be glorious white;
For in your presence, Jesus Christ
  There is no lack of light.

Nestling
[*For, Michael Ray*]

My little downy eagle,
How swift have flown the days
Since you were but a chick;
But now the time has come
For you to try your wings.
Sooner or later you will have to leave the nest,
For in time it will crumble and turn to dust;
But out there a new world
Awaits the beating of your wings.

You must exercise them soon—
Wings unused become atrophied,
And unable to fly.
Once you leave the nest you will grow stronger
As you ride upon the air.
The wind itself will help to bear you up
* And give you rest.*

Oh my little fledgling—
Why do you fear and tremble so?
Out there your destiny awaits;
If you diligently seek you will find.
Ask and it will be given.
Knock, and the doors of opportunity
Will be opened unto you.
Do not fear to take the first step.
I am with you always,
To help and guide you.
I will comfort you.

If you fall, I will be underneath you
To help stay you up upon the wind
When trouble comes I will be your
Sanctuary of peace and rest,
Until you're strong,
And confident enough to take the air again—
To finish your journey o'er the sea of life
Unto the golden shore that waits
Beyond the doors of time.

Dreams

The dreams of young children
 Are simple and sweet.
Dreams of bright, shiny new toys
 And ice cream to eat;
But as young hearts grow older
 Dreams become more intense.
Hopes and wishes grow stronger,
 Magnified by the sense
Of adolescent fires burning,
 Bringing stress to their lives—
Friction building up pressure,
 Escalating their drives.

Dreams then, must become channels—
  Vents to let off the steam,
Else young lives may shipwreck
  In foolish extreme.
Ere young hearts lose hope
  In dreams unfulfilled,
They must try on patience
  And in love be instilled.
So with others their dreams
  Can freely be shared—
Building a foundation
  On knowing they cared.

Cared enough to help others
  Find faith for their dreams.
Laying down aspirations
  For their own little schemes.
Giving hope to all people
  And help for their need—
Concerned, motivated,
  To be good friends indeed.
We find the secret of living
  When this goal we pursue.
Love makes life well worth living
  And our dreams all come true.

The Love Flowers

Once upon a glorious quest
 I chanced upon a garden.
Seeing a man nearby, I called,
 "Oh sir! I beg your pardon;
Do you know this ancient garden
 To whom does it belong?
I fear I may have lost my way,
 And the turn I made was wrong."

""Tis the garden of the King," he said
 In a voice spoke mute and low.
"In the valley of the sun,
 Where the love flowers grow.
It was once very beautiful
 When the king tended its needs,
But alas! You see the garden,
 Sore neglected, full of weeds."

When he spoke about the king,
   My heart skipped a beat.
My quest resolved to meet this king,
   And worship at his feet.
"Oh SIR!," I cried, "Please tell me more.
   Can you provide a clue?
I wish to meet this glorious king
   Tell me, what must I do?"

His silence grew oppressive,
   I wondered if he'd heard at all.
He gazed forlornly past the trees,
   Over the broken wall.
At last he turned and faced me
   And spoke these words in haste,
"The king no longer tends these grounds.
   You see his garden—it's a waste!

The king left to build a kingdom,
   And let the garden out to men.
He left instructions for its tending
   Written by his royal pen,
But the men he hired were evil,
   Rogues, from their early youth.
They brought the garden to its ruin.
   'Tis a shame! Forsooth!

"They refused the king's instruction,
    Would not heed his written word.
In the garden they were riotous
    Worst tumult I ever heard.
The poor little love flowers
    Just hung their heads in shame.
They had to give their precious fruit
    To those evil ones who came."

The king sent an envoy
    To collect some of their fruits,
But the soft and tender love flowers
    Had Been ravished by those brutes
They set upon those servants
    With shouts of evil glee,
Till the servants, sorely beaten,
    Were finally forced to flee.

Then the king sent his only child
    Beloved...his only begotten one.
'When they see my flesh and blood' he said
    'They will respect my son.'
But as he passed the garden gate
    They cried, 'Look! It is the heir!
Come, let's do away with him.
    We'll own it all, free and clear!'

They came and took the king's own son
   From the garden where he tread,
And did not cease to torture him
   Until he was quite dead.
But when they laid him in the grave
   Somehow the stone was rolled away.
Some said they saw him come to life
   And vow to return someday.

He'll put to death those evil men
   Whose acts have sealed their doom.
The trump' will sound! The KING will come!,
   And restore the garden from its gloom.
He'll pull the weeds with tender care,
   And trim and prune each bloom.
Then, the Love Flowers will blossom again,
   In triumph, o'er an empty tomb."

Illusion of Love
[*A Traditional Sonnet*]

Illusion of love, cloaked in deception,
Hid behind your opaque masque of false smiles;
Cunningly you spoke in dark encryption,
And seduced me with kisses, myths and wiles.
My heart was lonely, chasing endless goals,
Hoping to find a coalescing friend
With whom to intimately bond our souls
Unwary of the snare you hid within.

You stole my passion; Then filled me with ire,
Walking away with a wave of your hand.
You traitorous, lewd spurner of my fire;
You took my hopes and crushed them on time's sand.
  I gave you my trust—life—my very breath;
  And you gave me a path that leads to death.

A Hat-full of Rain

He grew up and only, the one child they had;
Love smothered by mother, rejected by dad.
He loathed the brown bottle that made life so sad.

So with the turning of sixteen plus one,
He forsook his parents for what they had done,
And lived as a loner—A world to be won.

But hope turned to ashes when he failed to find
The love that he sought, and a cloud silver lined,
So he too turned to drink for solace of mind.

Then wrapped in a stupor to help ease the pain,
He squandered his whole life, and labored in vain,
For the taste of cheap wine, and a hat full of rain.

Freedom's Foundation

"In God We Trust !"
Our motto speaks so plain.
For this great cause the valiant bore their pain.
These words penned by our founders still recall
Our freedom forged at Independence Hall—
Drawn up and signed in blood of loyals slain.

Our flag flies o'er the amber waves of grain.
The Statue of Liberty still stands tall.
These symbols of our strength declare to all
"In God We Trust !"

To throw away God's trust would be insane,
For only by his grace do we remain,
Land of Liberty and Justice For All.
To spurn God's love would cause our nations fall.
Pray congress will see and still proclaim,
"In God We Trust !"

50

Joyous Bird

If I could choose to be a bird,
What would I choose to be?
Would I be a Robin,
Or a tiny Chickadee?
Would I be an eagle
Soaring in the lofty sky?
Or would I be a Whip-or-will
With its lonesome, haunting cry?

No! Let me be a mocking bird
That's what I want to be.
For it can sing the sweetest songs
In mock diversity.
God gave that bird a gift to sing
All sorts of melodies
So sweet, I swear, that I can hear
The angel's harmonies.

Lord let my heart be as full of song
As the mocker's gray white breast.
Let me possess the mocker's joy
So when I'm put to test.
I can face adversity
In song from day to day
And be prepared for every trial
That wants to come my way.

A Taste of Love

When I first heard that you loved me,
And you enticed my hand with treats;
I passed you by and scorned your love—
I Strolled on down the broad dark street,
Seeking the treasures of the world—
Much richer things, I thought I'd find.
"I'll stand on my own two feet." I said,
"I'll rule my life with my own mind."

But the house I built was made of sand.
Strong winds and waves came to prevail.
I saw my house could not remain—
Knew it was destined soon to fail.
Then I learned, I could not stand alone;
Without your love I could not live.
So I returned and sought you out,
And found you willing to forgive.

I embraced your warm amazing love.
Your sweet voice spoke oh so unique.
I caught the sweetest scent of heaven,
In every word I heard you speak.
Because your grace could still be found
The day I set my heart to seek,
I found a taste of God's own love,
As tears ran slowly down my cheek.

Poets Renown

Poets explore the reaches of their dreams,
Sifting ideas on rhymed and metered line;
Seeking perchance a thought from which it seems
Concepts may be cut out and polished fine;
Making souls laugh or drown in tragic tears
When they plant words like wheat on fertile ground;
Raising up songs so sweet they last for years,
Traveling the earth in waves of subtle sound.

Listen! Feel the flowing rhythmic gait,
Riding on steeds of myth set loose from id.
Bound for the realm of truth that yet awaits
To be discovered where the poets hid
    Succulent bits of worlds both right and wrong
    Which they expertly crafted in their song.

Adventurer

My trek began at childhood
  And darkness was the rule.
Threats, fights, and timidity
  Were all taught at my school.

Past graveyards of long dead men
  Where the hounds of adversity bark,
I danced to the music,
  Of the orchestra of dark.

Until one day I met someone
  At a fork in the road.
"Come...Stop and talk awhile," he said,
  "And rest your heavy load."

He pointed to a narrow way
  Leading upwards to a hill,
A hill illumined with soft pale light
  That bade me peace be still.

As I gazed upon a sacred scene
From a time so long ago,
My mind began to understand—
My heart began to know.

I had suddenly turned a bend,
Trouble and worry were gone.
Darkness and clouds had flown,
Replaced by golden dawn.

Skies were not as dark as before,
But a paler shade of blue.
My strength and courage were renewed,
By the sunlight streaming through.

New companions—champions of peace,
And harmonic fragrance filled the air.
I knew I could face life squarely;
There was nothing left to fear.

Never again will I inhabit
Wild places I have known.
Life has become an adventure;
Bravely I walk on...

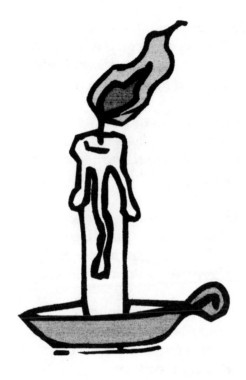

A Noble Knight's Work

I rode from the king's stately castle—
My tried and true sword by my side.
The kings rations were in my saddlebags
And a spectral companion my guide.
"'Neath the weight of my armor, a warm cloak
Would protect me from cold winter's wind
My foot-gear was leather—Covered in iron—
And jointed to easily bend.

"Head for the towns beyond the wall," I said,
"It will take us three days to arrive.
"I must post the king's message to mankind,
"That the prince is not dead, but alive!"
He is home from the heinous "Mother of Wars"
With gifts from the victory he won.
He reigns again on his father's throne—
The battle is over and done.

We'll ride in the light of the warm, bright sun—
Post guard through the night and beware.
Thus avoiding the creatures of darkness
Who drag lost souls to their lair
There are brutes still searching the valleys
For subjects who fall easy prey.
But they usually travel in darkness,
And shun the bright light of the day.

I spurred my strong steed on till evening
Till he sighed from the grueling gait.
Then I stopped by the road for a rest—
To eat, and 'til morning to wait.
We were deep in a valley of shadows.
And I knew danger was lurking near.
In the distance I saw circling vultures.
And a howling of wolves I could hear.

I ate the king's bread and drank of his wine
As I warily watched o'er the land
I reached for my sword, and suddenly,
A small bird flew right in my hand.
I gently cupped my hands 'round its form—
So beautiful, lithe and unique.
I gently caressed its trembling warmth
Then startled, I heard it speak.

"I am weary from fleeing the darkness—
A mother of babies am I.
In my search for my family's provisions
I got lost and am ready to die."
I need someone's help to find strength.", she said,
I'm too weak to fly any more.
I'm ready to quit and be done with this life,
My wings feel so heavy and sore."

Alarmed at the tears in her voice, I sighed.
Concern for this creature welled up.
I felt in my heart, affectionate love
From springs of emotions erupt.
I reached in my store of bountiful food,
And gave her the drink and bread of kings.
I talked sweet to her in comforting tones,
And rubbed healing balm on her wings.

She drank in new wine of mercy and joy.
And I watched her bounce back like a spring.
I fed her until she wanted no more,
Then satisfied, and slaked...she sang.
The purest melody poured out of her heart.
There were no tears or pain in her voice.
That song so refreshed and thrilled me,
I began to dance and rejoice.

I held her there through the long winter night,
But heartache came swift with the dawn.
I open my hands and to my surprise,
On strong beating wings she was gone.
As I ride through the forest I see her.
Just a glance as I travel along.
I can still hear her song in the moonlight,
As my quest moves relentlessly on...

At the Sound of the Tone

Hello!
You have reached nine, four, three—
  Four, three, three, two,
The home of Edwin,
  Becky and Sue.

If you are a salesman,
  Let me tell you we're broke.
I couldn't buy a flea a bonnet,
  And that ain't no joke.

Now if it's a survey
  You've got on your mind,
I can't take your call,
  I just don't have the time.

But my friend Leroy Smith,
  He just loves to do these;
If you will call him
  I'm sure he'd be pleased.

If you're a bill collector,
  The checks in the mail,
But I could only send half,
  You see, my wife is in jail.

The neighbor shot my dog,
  And Sue called raisin' heck
She's out of the hospital,
  But needs to pay for her wreck.

If you're a crank caller
  And you're still on the line,
Then the calls already traced—
  We caught you this time.

If you got a wrong number,
  I'm sure you hung up the phone;
But, if you're still there,
  Then just wait for the tone.

Be prepared to give your name,
  Address and occupation.
And state your reason for calling
  Without hesitation.

If you're a friend, relative,
  Or grand prize coordinator,
Speak your number real clear,
  And I'll call you back later.

If you're still there, you're sure persistent,
  So talk at the sound of the tone.
If I am home, and if I am listening,
  I may even pick up the phone...

The Golden Years

All the former ties are broken.
All the "Good-ol'-Boys" have gone.
Life's events have turned to history,
And old friends that I have known
Are lost beyond the miles of life
That cannot be retraced.
Although, the memories linger
Of hard-times I have faced.

Where will my journey take me?
What lies beyond the bend?
Who knows what fate awaits me,
Or where the road will end?
How can I know what steps to choose
That lead to good ahead?
What steps to completely avoid
To detour fear and dread?

When strangers come to greet me,
Will they be friend or foe?
I'll trust my heart to help discern,
And sift their words to know.
The only one I truly trust
Is risen from the dead.
I'll talk with him, and trust his word
For the miles that lie ahead.

If I Had Time

*If I Had Time
I'd write extraordinary rhyme
Or find a mountain I could scale;
Then I'd board ship and slowly sail
To distant lands across the deep
In search of memories I could keep.
I'd savor love, I'd laugh—I'd weep—
If I Had Time*

*Sky diving is a flying leap—
A commendable endeavor;
But the type of thing I would avoid
Lest my person be destroyed.
Dare-devils like to do or die. NOT I!
They fling their taunt, "It's now or never!"
But I for one would like to live...forever,
If I Had Time*

Liberty
[Dedicated to those who would
set Old Glory aflame]

Our forebears left their native homes
To come to this fair shore,
Seeking a state of liberty
Men never knew before.

They bravely crossed the stormy sea
In wooden ships with sails—
Fought bloody wars for the liberty
Which America proudly hails.

When Betsy Ross with thread in hand,
With stars and stripes the cloth adorned;
From aching hands and fingers sore
"Old Glory," our dear flag was born.

Americans love their liberty;
They court her with ardor.
Her statue, given to us by France
Stands tall in New York Harbor.

Her upraised torch is brightly lit
For all the world to see
How much we cherish freedom in
This land of liberty.

But should the torch burn bright enough
To set our flag aflame;
Allowing some to spurn our land
Which we so proudly claim?

When liberty can burn the flag,
"Old Glory" cannot reign.
Our liberty will turn to rust—
Only ashes will remain.

A Knight's Delight

Sir Lancelot rode
　From his castle abode
　To the realm of his cultural peers.
Big Charger, his steed,
　Was renowned for his speed,
　Standing twenty hands tall when he rears.

As he crossed the deep moat,
　Lance cleared-up his throat
　And made mental notes for his spiel.
For, this day he would stand
　In the midst of a band,
　Who wrought words like smithy's at steel.

He arrived at the place
  With a smile on his face,
  Mulling words like, admire and endear.
For, he pined to delight
  That lady of light,
  The princess of dawn, Guinevere.

So, challenging fate,
  He swung through the gate
  And took up his place at the table;
Along with the rest,
  Who were known as the best
  Of the ready, willing and able.

Ready to pick up the glove
  Of the hawk for the dove,
  And go forth to each worthy deed;
Lance listened, elated,
  As their tales they related,
  And to each feat of fame he took heed.

Lance heard chatter cease
  While he told out his piece,
  Then he caught a shy, feminine look.
Her teary eyes blurry,
  Guinevere, looked down demurely,
  And buried her nose in a book.

Trying to hide her delight
That she felt for this knight,
Who had rescued herself from grave harm.
"Beware those eyes!"
Growled Sir Buckingham Wise,
"You know she belongs to Prince John."

His words fell on deaf ears;
Foolish love never hears;
Lance bade him to shush and depart.
Guin's eyes, limpid pools,
Turned men into fools,
But Lance sought to win her fair heart.

At the end of the meet,
With the fire at low heat,
The knights drifted out one by one;
Taking Guinevere's hand,
Lance bade her to stand,
And they left with the slow setting sun.

Riding swift through the night,
They beheld a great sight,
A giant, floating orb made of gold.
They were both struck with awe
At this marvel they saw
And Lance sought Guin's hand for to hold.

They talked in quiet whispers,
  Like prayers said at vespers,
  While Lance gazed at her lovely face.
The ache of their need
  Made them draw close indeed,
  And Lance felt his blood start to race.

"I must be gone," he said,
  "Ere this goes to my head,
  And I do something rash I'll regret."
But, in quiet compassion,
  They both slaked their passion
  With sweets Lance will never forget.

Now Guinevere's gone,
  Yet her scent lingers on,
  From the perfume she wore on that night.
And the painful reminder
  That Prince John still owns her—
  This fairest princess of light.

Poor Lance is heartbroken
  For he has but a token,
  To remember the pain of love's bite.
Fate has been so unkind,
  Lance knows he'll ne'er find
  Another such knight's delight.

Love, Two, Three

One, Eros:
When I first met love,
  It was at ground zero.
I was bold and dashing—
  Trying to play hero.
Lusting with a physical,
  Primal, yearning for a mate.
This love was vain and vulgar;
  Tinged with jealousy and hate.
There were sweethearts to pursue,
  And rivals to defeat,
Lest they come to steal your love,
  And leave you incomplete.
This love can never satisfy,
  It just plays an empty part.
"Surely something else," I said,
  "Will fill this lonesome heart."

Two, Philos:
I left the mortal state,
  Looking for what would make me whole.
I entered a higher plane,
  And discovered love of soul.
You and I became accompliced
  In a sweet fraternal bond.
Emotions swept like ripples
  On a quiet secluded pond.
Loving like a friend or sibling,
  With no malevolent intent.
Then endurance reached its limit,
  And began this subtle hint.
"My friend, I love you just like family,
  But I say in fervent heat,
Touch my mate, property, or money,
  And you're dead meat."

Three, Agapè :

Above the astral plane of soul
  Is where true love is found,
Coming down from the Father of Lights
  Like a harmonic, peaceful sound.
This love is patient, not demanding,
  Always gentle—always kind.
Love that shows concern for others,
  Always wise, and never blind.
Dwelling deep within the psyche
  It wells from eternal springs.
It thinks only of your happiness,
  And never dotes on earthly things.
I want you to know, this gentle heart
  Is full of love that's true—
Love, self sacrificing and willing,
  And it's this love I have for you.

Perpetual Embrace
[*A Traditional Sonnet*]

I saw them standing in the church garden.
Locked in each others limbs so firm and tight.
Certain they were alone and well hidden,
In faintly, glowing, paleness of twilight.
She leaned back, as if her mood was playful,
As his limbs circled 'round her lovely waist,
Holding her quite firm, and yet so gentle;
Almost afraid, because she was still chaste.

They stood there softly swaying in the breeze,
Dancing to the wind's mournful melody.
I gazed upon these seeming Siamese,
And wished we could become a parody;
Then suddenly you laughed and broke the spell
Of watching oaks embracing in the dell.

The Saga of Adeena and Orin

'Twas Adeena and Orin of Whispering Key,
Came riding sea horses o'er shimmering sea.
'Tween noontime and midnight their journey did last
While threatening, cumulus, dark shadows cast.

Skys finally clearing, the moon led them ashore;
Apprehensive, weary, and soaked to the core.
Orin searched out flint and wood, and ignited a pyre.
Adeena dried their clothes in the heat of the fire.

Cuddling together they slept on the beach,
Till rudely awakened by a gull's piercing screech.
They broke fast on berries Orin found in the bush,
Then set off in search of the evil King Krush.

Krush had a challis of diamonds and gold—
'Twas said from the God, "Logos" was stole.
The challis was enchanted and to use it for ale,
Woke the lips of the drinker to weave a great tale.

Logos was the greatest teller of odes
And swore the thieves would be turned into toads;
But Adeena and Orin must beware of the guard,
Or they'd wind up locked in the Krush prison yard.

But, the quest they had taken, and they'd not give in,
Though they knew it might mean death in the end.
They crossed the Black Mountains,
    Castle spires rose in sight,
And black smoke, from the tower,
        Blocked the sun's light.

"Krush is making his afternoon sacrifice," Orin said.
"That tower's a one way trip to the land of the dead."
Adeena gripped Orin's hand and gave a low moan,
But Orin assured her, and urged gently on.

Adeena was known for her prowess in fight;
She had even defeated the strength of a Knight.
But, Krush was known as a mean, evil wizard
And Adeena loathed him like a slimy lizard.

At the forest edge, they watched the sun's last rays.
They waited for dark, for what seemed endless days.
At nightfall, Orin led the way to the moat;
Adeena worried about having no boat.

Suddenly Orin closed his eyes,
      chanting under his breath,
And they walked 'cross the water,
      as 'gators slept like death.
Climbing up the drawbridge, by way of the chain,
Orin stabbed the guard until he fell down slain.

Silently, they crept past the Doberman's lair,
As prickles of fear swept the nape of their hair.
Two more guards went down ere they were done.
They looked for more guards but found not a one.

Standing by Krush's chamber
      they heard his loud snore,
And in pale moonlight,
      the chalice gleamed by a door—
A door to the innermost sanctum of the castle,
Where Krush and the Queen were oft heard to hassle.

Creeping silently in,
      Orin put his sword to Krush's throat,
As he muttered under his breath, "Die you old goat."
Then, with one stroke he deftly cut off his head;
Grabbed the Chalice and to Adeena said:

"Put the head in a sack for proof and let's go.
We must away before anyone knows."
Reaching in a case they snatched up two knives;
If they were discovered, they would pay with their lives.

Adeena started stuffing the head in a sack
And saw dark blood run from the neck;
Losing her cool, she let out a scream,
And the head turned to a pillow...'twas only a dream.

Echoes of Time
[*A Traditional Sonnet*]

At dusk, sunset merges into twilight,
And we prepare to rest and dream till dawn.
Meanwhile the dusky raven takes her flight.
Till shadows cast by moon have come and gone,
The morning's dove mounts on his wings of white,
Continuing the trip to journey's end;
Where day once more will merge into the night,
At spiral's point just past the origin,

Oh how I wish I could turn back the years,
And amend mistakes while I yet live.
Cries of those I've hurt still sound in my ears;
I only hope someday they will forgive.
Who knows how long these flights of time will last,
To add onto the echoes from the past.

Gray Passage

There is a course of dreary gray
That wanders through a neutral zone.
Pounded by feet still traveling
To destinations yet unknown.
There is no truth—there is no lie,
That can be set in concrete there,
It is the task of time alone,
To slowly strip deception bare.

The bright apex becoming clear,
As miles appear, and disappear,
But then we stand appalled to see,
A beast—emerging from nadir!
The night attempts to hide with dark,
What day illumes with golden light
Until we see the precious truth,
And understand the goal in sight.

We look beyond the miles of gray,
And fear the haunting siren's call,
Compelling us into the grave,
The final resting place of all.
Is there a place beyond the black,
Where white will shine forever bright?
Faith says: "When night has come and gone,
Joy is made perfect in the light.

Black on White
[*A French Rondeau*]

In Black on White
the answer came,
Although the writing was the same—
Old words, I'd read and talked about;
But this time the meaning left no doubt.
To cloud the power of God's name;
To compromise creation's fame,
By tolerating false acclaim,
That tries to plant black lies throughout,
In Black on White

That spark of love blew into flame
As God's words of love for me became
A ROCK! A fortress of redoubt:
I plucked those lies and threw them out
When truth I heard God's word proclaim
In Black on White.

79

First Love
[*A Traditional Sonnet*]

Beyond the east the light came from the void
Spreading awareness to the sons of grace,
Who wisdom learned, till they became annoyed,
And looking back, beheld Night's lovely face.
Like fools they left their lofty mountain home,
Descending to the shadowed valley floor,
Chasing the wind till they, too tired to roam,
Returned, but found...someone had locked the door.

Sitting beside the gates they wept aloud.
And longed to have the love of wisdom flown.
They were a teary-eyed, repentant crowd,
Who now must travel on their way alone.
  With darkness lying heavy on their eyes,
  Lamenting for their lost love, paradise.

80

The Birth of Creation

Between the Night and Daylight, Morning was born,
Bringing up his red rays of Sunrise.
When Daylight turned to Night again, Evening came,
Bringing all her violet mist of twilight.

Growing up, Morning loved Evening with such passion,
It made the waters boil within the sea.
Their chosen family name, Children of Light,
Were all raised in rainbow colors of high fashion.

The Brotherhood of Fire was cheery red,
While the Sisters of the Sea were all in blue.
From their love the Golden Sun and Wind were born.
Who married the blue Daughters of the Sea.

The Sun and Wind, loving Blue Waters,
Brought the facts of life to birth.
And between the three of the them
Came forth the family Circle, we call Earth.

The Human Race

Creation Week, Creation Week,
With days of perfect seven;
Please, give us your dimensions
From Hades unto Heaven.
We want to know the whole of you
From now unto forever;
Are you a square, or are you Round?
How are you put together?

I am a sphere of such great size
You cannot comprehend
The measurement of all I AM
From beginning to the end;
But, listen close and I will try
To give you some idea
Of the corners of the cosmos
In my vast rotating sphere.

My top is in the center
  And my bottom's on the side;
I sit on top the mountain
  And watch the horses ride
From east to west around the clock
  As each tomorrow turns to past,
Until the final sunset
  Where the race will end at last.

Red horse of fire—Pale horse of air
  Over water—Over earth,
Have run the race of life and death
  Since creation gave them birth.
You stand up and cheer them on,
  And drink your cup of sin.
All you need is to— Believe!—
  Then bet on life to win.

Valentine

I could buy a million words
By a million other men,
But they could ne'er express the fire
Of emotions deep within;
To cast this light, 'tis myself
Must take the poet's pen
And dip it in the well of life
Where roots of love begin.
Then write the words that bubble forth
Ere they stale and pass away.
Quickly now! Capture the thoughts
And Soon, before you I lay
A work created from my heart
Of things I've wished to say
About life, joy, and eternal love
   On some glorious future day.

Meet the Author

Ronnie Bee,

is a native Georgian, who resides in Douglas County Georgia. He is a *Distinguished Member* of the *International Society of Poets*.

Ronnie's poems have been selected many times by the I.S.O.P for publication in their anthologies, and his poem "Poets Renown" was selected for an *Editor's Choice* award in their book *The Path Not Taken*, ISBN 1-57553-003-1.

Ronnie was selected as Poet Laureate for the year 1992-93, by Douglas Poets in Focus, a satellite of the *Douglas County Cultural Arts Council*.

Ronnie is an *associate* in the Computer Science field, and is experienced in many areas of Computers, Technical Services, and Information Processing Services.

Ronnie has a deep love for poetry and music. He says, "Some poems are not meant to be understood, but are simply to be read for the pure enjoyment of reading. Other poems express deep feelings of emotions, and are almost like a personal glimpse into the inner recesses of the poet's soul. A good poem can bring you tears of sadness, warmth of love, laughter, or even feelings of cruelty and deep despair, to your own psyche."

Ronnie strives for excellence in all his endeavors.

To order additional copies of **Illusions of Truth,** complete the information below.

Ship to: (please print)

Name _____

Address _____

City, State, Zip _____

Day phone _____

_____ copies of *Illusions of Truth* @ $9.95 each $ _____

Postage and handling @ $3.00 per book $ _____

GA residents add 6% tax $ _____

Total amount enclosed $ _____

*Make checks payable to **Honeybee Publishing Co.***

Send to: P.O. Box 941
Douglasville, GA 30133-0941

To order additional copies of **Illusions of Truth,** complete the information below.

Ship to: (please print)

Name _____

Address _____

City, State, Zip _____

Day phone _____

_____ copies of *Illusions of Truth* @ $9.95 each $ _____

Postage and handling @ $3.00 per book $ _____

GA residents add 6% tax $ _____

Total amount enclosed $ _____

*Make checks payable to **Honeybee Publishing Co.***

Send to: P.O. Box 941
Douglasville, GA 30133-0941